Willem de Kooning:
a portrait

# Bert Schierbeek

# Willem de Kooning:
# a portrait

Introduction
Karin Evers en Guido Walraven

Menken Kasander & Wigman Uitgevers
Leiden
2005

© 1969/2005 Erven Bert Schierbeek

Introduction: © 2005 Karin Evers, Guido Walraven

Translation introduction DU/EN: Ton Broos

Editing: Camiel Hamans

ISBN 9781532883378

www.mkw-uitgevers.nl

## Introduction

Leafing through collected works of Bert Schierbeek (1918–1996), one will come across countless poems that have a relation to the visual arts. Out of sheer admiration or personal affection, the poet was inspired by the works of diverse artists like Shinkichi Tajiri, Pierre van Soest and Frank Lodeizen, as well as Loes van der Horst, Jan Sierhuis and Guillaume Leroy; in other words: by images, abstract graphics, large installations in public spaces, colorful canvases by mainly Dutch artists who crossed his path.

But often the reverse also happened: many painters, sculptors, photographers and filmmakers took Schierbeek's poems as a starting point for their creations. The most remarkable example of this is the painter Jef Diederen, who was so totally impressed by Schierbeek's poem *Ezel mijn bewoner* (Donkey my inhabitant) that he was hard to stop: a series of 85 drawings and gouaches was the result.

That mutual influence has resulted in a beautiful collection of collaborations, starting in 1954 with *Het bloed stroomt door* (The Blood keeps flowing), a text edition by Bert Schierbeek, accompanied by ten black and white drawings by Karel Appel. Their friendship dated from the early fifties, when Bert Schierbeek on his Parisian scouting trips, visited Appel's studio at Rue Santeuil. In later years he would also work together with Lotti van der Gaag and Corneille, whom he also met there.

It is perhaps less known that Schierbeek showed his affinity to the visual arts not only in his poetry, but also in his prose texts. He opened exhibitions, did interviews with artists, and wrote introductions to catalogs. For those activities he was widely praised. For example, reviewing the catalog *De kleur van Leo Schatz* (Leo Schatz' Color, 1989) in his 'Journaille-column' in Amsterdam newspaper *Het Parool*, Jan Vrijman paid him a compliment. 'See, that's the way to do it,' asserted Jan Vrijman pointedly. 'His story and the beautiful reproductions drove me irresistibly towards the exhibition.' Vrijman thought that Schierbeek was 'the' person to write about art. And he was not alone in that. The question remains how that came about. An often-heard answer was: Schierbeek was such an excellent observer. 'You could hear him looking at things,' Diederen explained. 'When driving through the countryside, he would take in everything. Like a child looking at things for the first time. He would loudly read slogans from billboards or trucks. Look, there goes International Movers, he would shout enthusiastically.'

Edy de Wilde, former director of the Stedelijk Museum in Amsterdam, noticed Schierbeek's keen eye by chance. In 1939, during mobilization prior to World War II, they had gotten to know each other. They would talk for hours and dream along the Hoornse Hop, an inlet from the IJsselmeer lake. De Wilde recalled later: 'The way Bert used to look at the light on the clouds, or a little ship sailing, struck me immediately. I felt a certain kinship in that.'

Willem Sandberg, Edy de Wilde's predecessor in the Stedelijk Museum, also saw Schierbeek's qualities early

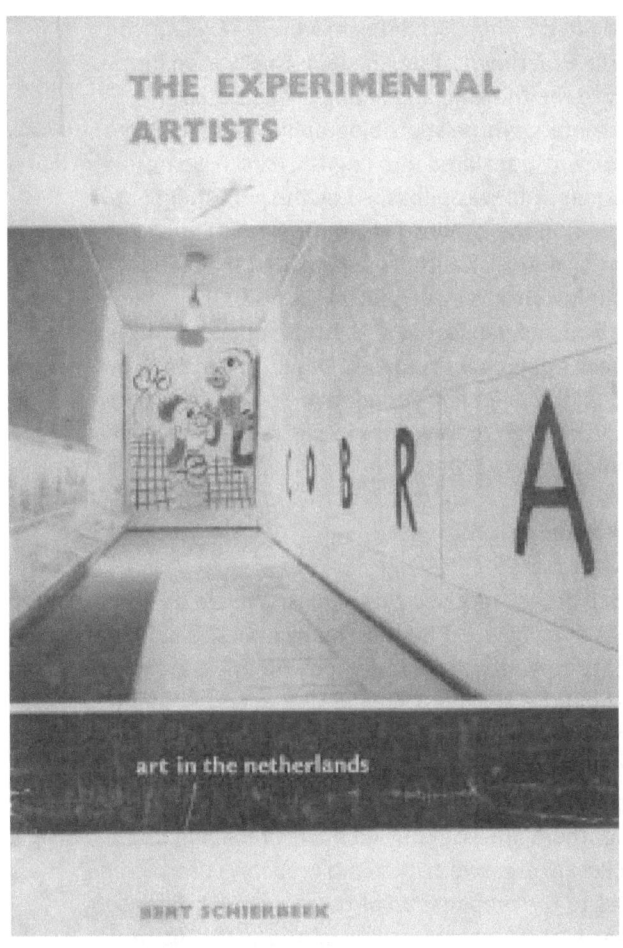

THE EXPERIMENTAL
ARTISTS

COBRA

art in the netherlands

BERT SCHIERBEEK

*Schierbeek's introduction to the thinking and acting of
the Dutch Cobra-painters (1964)*

on. Instigated by him, Schierbeek wrote *De Experimen-*
*telen* (The Experimentalists) in 1964. This was an introduction to the thinking and acting of the Dutch
Cobra-painters, whose short biographies were included.
The book was translated into English, French, Spanish
and German, and was published by the publishing house
Meulenhoff in their series 'Arts in the Netherlands'. Pub-
lications by different authors appeared in that series,
about for instance Wessel Couzijn, De Stijl, J.B. Jongkind,
neo-realism and Van Dongen. They must have liked
Schierbeek's approach, because a request was made by
Bloemena of Meulenhoff for another book in the series.
Did he want to go to New York to portray painter Willem
de Kooning (1904–1997)?

**King De Kooning**

When Schierbeek received this request, Willem de Kooning was already world famous. Many critics called him
the greatest painter in contemporary America. In fact, at
new exhibitions the question had shifted to whether De
Kooning was already past his prime. That can be gath-
ered from the survived folder with reviews and articles
that Schierbeek was reading prior to his visit to De
Kooning. There are essays by Clement Greenberg and
Harold Rosenberg, two critics who probably contributed
the most to the propagation of the movement described
by them as 'abstract expressionism' and 'action painting'. This movement emerged at the end of the forties
and flourished in the fifties. Besides Willem de Kooning,
it includes Jackson Pollock, Mark Rothko, Barnett New-
man, Franz Kline and Robert Motherwell. Schierbeek

also had pieces by Thomas Hess, who, when writing about abstract-expressionists, was especially focused on Willem de Kooning.

Initially there was a strong rivalry between Jackson Pollock and Willem de Kooning, which was not limited to their artistic skills, but also involved women and alcohol. After Pollock died in a car accident in 1956, De Kooning was regarded as the most prominent painter of abstract expressionism.

It was obvious to refer to the meaning of his regal name: 'koning' and 'king'. Lee Hall even used the metaphor of the coronation, the happenings in the king-dom and the death of the king as base for the structure of her book *Elaine and Bill, Portrait of a Marriage: the Lives of Willem and Elaine De Kooning* (1993). 'Queen' Elaine Fried, with whom Willem de Kooning lived to-gether for a long time, made great efforts to enlarge the fame of the painter. One of the intrigues at the court was that Elaine had an affair with Thomas Hess and wrote about De Kooning in the art magazine of which Hess was the editor.

At the time that Schierbeek wants to visit De Kooning, much has changed in the painter's life. Movements and hypes in the art world rapidly follow each other. The at-tention moves from abstract expressionism to pop art, and the abstract-expressionists are going their own way. De Kooning has replaced the busy city of New York for rural Long Island, where many things remind him in a number of ways of the country of his birth, as Schier-beek reports extensively. Although even now the repeat-ing themes in his works and his handicraft provide for continuity in his work, his new direction brings many changes.

From 1955 onwards, De Kooning started a number of highly abstracted urban landscapes that became more and more rural in character, and also had the sea as subject, the longer he stayed in the Hamptons on Long Island. In the sixties, however, he again made a series of paintings of women. When Schierbeek comes to visit, female and other figures, abstracted landscapes and sea views dominate.

Whether De Kooning was directly involved in his own public relations, or whether he preferred to leave this to people in his direct surroundings, it is obvious that he above all preferred to paint. That was already the case during the wild years in Manhattan with friends and alcohol. Since his departure to Long Island, he often worked seven days a week, which at first hindered Schierbeek, but could be nicely observed by him later.

**A book or no book**

Interviewing De Kooning was not as easy as initially thought. In a letter to Jan Gerhard Toonder in January 1967, Margreetje, Schierbeek's wife at the time, writes: 'Bert has gone to Willem de Kooning for a few days – at first he sounded more like William the Silent – impossible to get him on the phone or to make an appointment with him. After a lot of modest and respectful waiting, Bert finally got so angry that he demanded over the phone (and fortunately he got the boss himself on the line) a definitive answer: a book or no book. And the poor man, who kept postponing because his painting

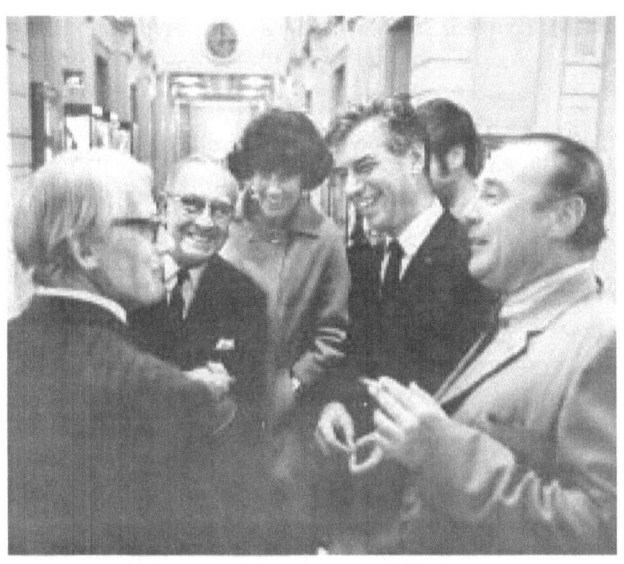

*Stedelijk Museum 1968, left to right: Willem de Kooning,
Jan Heyligers, Nono Reinhold, Edy de Wilde,
Bert Schierbeek*

"bugged" him so much, seemed hardly aware of what it was all about. Now everything is beautiful and wonderful. Bert is enormously excited. They talk days and nights and surely wash down a glass or two in between. In short, it promises to be a beautiful book.'

However, a book never materialized. There was a typescript, entitled *Willem de Kooning: a portrait* that was ready for the typesetter. This text was entirely in English, but a previous incomplete version, which was found in Schierbeek's estate, consists of a mixture of English and Dutch. It is very likely that Schierbeek's American friend Charles McGeehan, who translated much of Schierbeek's works, translated the Dutch and corrected the English. The strange thing is that this apparently happened after the first retrospective of De Kooning, organized in the Stedelijk Museum in 1968. A few fragments from Schierbeek's text had been included in the catalog, while the complete book was announced for 1969. In the mainly English text, a few Dutch lines pop up occasionally: 'En vergenoegd lachend voegt hij eraan toe: "Humor sneaks in."'

The catalog also has an introduction by Thomas Hess, who, like Schierbeek, was one of the speakers at the opening of the exhibition, organized by the then director Edy de Wilde. De Kooning himself was also there, back in the Netherlands for the first time since his departure for America. At that moment there did not seem to be a problem, but when Schierbeek continued to work on the manuscript and a translation was made, some frustration emerged. The story goes that De Kooning, who could behave other-worldly and absent minded, had not completely realized that Schierbeek had come for a serious publication. Thomas Hess didn't seem to be impressed by Schierbeek's approach. Edy de Wilde believes that Hess thought it to be superficial, and that Schierbeek had made it too easy for himself. Schierbeek thought that Hess was afraid that he would turn De Kooning too much into a 'Dutch painter'. Similarly, abstract expressionism had been branded as a typical American movement, the first one that could measure up to European schools in painting, and the first one that would indicate that New York had become the center of the art world, succeeding Paris.

Besides Hess, also Fourcade, the gallery owner of De Koonings at the time, was active in guarding the image of the American master. He prevented the publication of a monograph about De Kooning, because he thought that the painter deserved a better-known author.

It remains unclear what happened at the editors' desk, but it is a fact that publisher Meulenhoff abandoned the project entirely. Since then, the typescript, as well as Schierbeek's copy, had been lost. Until two years after his death, in 1998, the long lost manuscript was found among the author's papers. The 2005 Willem de Kooning retrospective at the Kunsthal in Rotterdam, his birthplace, seems the perfect occasion to finally publish Schierbeek's text.

Karin Evers
Guido Walraven

Willem de Kooning

A portrait ...

by Bert Schierbeek

> Nothing is positive about art except
> that it is a word.
>
> The artist takes art as he finds it.
>
> Art becomes a way to avoid a way.
>
> Forms ought to have the emotion of a
> concrete experience. For instance,
> I am very happy that grass is green.

These statements were made by Willem de Kooning, the American
painter, born in Rotterdam, now 64 years of age. He has also
been living in and around New York for over forty years. For
the last ten years he has been one of the most illustrious of
American painters, "the grey-locked dean of abstract expressionism".
His influence on American painting between the two world wars
and thereafter is in many respects comparable with that of
Pablo Picasso on the European scene. His ........ personality
and still exerted a catalysing effect on his surroundings and
his artist friends.

*First page of the typescript of Bert Schierbeek*

14

*Nothing is positive about art except that it is a word.*
*The artist takes art as he finds it.*
*Art becomes a way to avoid a way.*
*Forms ought to have the emotion of a concrete experi-*
*ence. For instance: I am very happy that grass is green.*


These statements were made by Willem de Kooning, the American painter, born in Rotterdam, now 64 years of age. He has been living in and around New York for over forty years. For the last ten years he has been one of the most illustrious of American painters, 'the grey-looked dean of abstract expressionism'.

His influence on American painting between the two world wars and thereafter is in many respects comparable with that of Pablo Picasso on the European scene. His personality and skill exerted a catalyzing effect on his surroundings and his artist friends.

De Kooning was twenty-two when he sailed to America. For ten years he had attended the night-courses of de *Academie voor Beeldende Kunsten en Techniese Wetenschappen* (The Academy for Applied Arts and Design) in Rotterdam. He did that upon the advice of Jan and Jaap Gidding, 'painters and decorators', with whom he had taken up employment after elementary school.

To New York he brought along his giftedness, his skill, and his familiarity with European painting. From his mother, a headstrong, willful and domineering woman, he got his perseverance and the will to do something unique, without making any concessions to the outside world.

'I want to be the greatest artist, the greatest lover and the greatest drinker.'

These he succeeded in splendidly, though not exactly as his mother had foreseen or intended.

From his father he fell heir to unconcern, mobility, and the unflinching swagger to battle through the toughest of situations... and maybe a kind of diffidence and shyness as well.

His parents separated, so at an early age he was learning to look at life from two sides.

'The ambiguity of reality' has always played a great role in his work and his statements.

His grey head has something catlike about it and this is one cat you can't put into anyone's bag.

'What I see is a glimpse, a glimpse of reality, and that glimpse is the essence of my reality, and I'm that special part of it and all. So what I make out of it must be real.'

But sometimes months could slip by before he could get his 'glimpse' onto canvas, for nothing is easy. And after some such months he would throw the irksome canvas into a corner and despair and drink and drink too much. Then the confrontation could begin anew and be worked out in an hour and he could set it aside. He'd set it aside and say that it was finished, that is: finished forever... Yet it is said that, for those who possess works of his, it is not advisable, anymore, to lend him these paintings, because one can never be certain that he won't start to 'finish' them again.

'I'm not ready yet,' is proverbial of De Kooning. He has turned down several offers for exhibitions.

He has given a good deal of thought to the problems and possibilities of painting, and he doesn't stuff his thoughts under the sofa or the rug. That, in part, explains for the great influence he had on his artistic milieu.

The first contact I had with him was by telephone. We had made the appointment to meet at his place.

'Now listen,' he said, 'you take the 2:07 train of the Long Island Railroad this afternoon, leaving from Grand Central to Montauk. You take that train and you sit quiet, for people who know sit quiet on that train. There are many Hamptons... There's West Hampton, Hampton, Hampton's Bay, but you sit quiet, and when you see *East* Hampton you get off... and I'll be there...'

A youthful, sonorous voice from East Hampton, Long Island, three hours by train from New York. De Kooning had been living there for ten years.

As the train left New York progressively behind, I was coming right back into a Dutch landscape. Rivers, woods, lakes, dunes. Pollock had lived and worked there, so had Franz Kline; and Harold Rosenberg still lives there, as does Saul Steinberg.

Elaine de Kooning, herself a good painter, to whom De Kooning was married in 1943 and from whom he is now divorced, described *her* first meeting with him as follows:

'I met Bill in a bar in 1936. I thought he had seaman's eyes that seemed as if they were staring at very wide spaces all day. He had an inhuman look - vacant, limpid, angelic. I visited his studio several days later with a friend. It was the cleanest place I ever saw in my life. It had painted gray floors, white walls, one table, one bed, four chairs, one easel, one fantastically good phono-graph that cost $ 800 when he was only making twenty-two dollars a week, and one painting - a man - on the easel. The whole effect was that this man was great.'

Upon the platform at East Hampton stood De Kooning. A smallish, broad-shouldered man whose bearing re-minded me of the Dutch architect, Gerrit Rietveld. He too had the same bright blue-grey eyes, which really seemed to be empty, at least to be a bit suggestive of expectancy with remoteness, but also of the confidence of being able to overcome this prospect. And yet there was also something vulnerable in his eyes. But then we shook hands; and his grip was firm, and his look was open. His grey forelock hung lank over his forehead. His large right hand stroked it back now and then.

'You know, last week I couldn't receive you,' he was saying in an apologetic tone, 'because there's a painting I'm working on now that's really bugging me - I mean it.'
   The next day I could see that with my own eyes.
   But first we went to a restaurant in West Hampton for dinner.
   'D'you like wild duck?'
   And without waiting for an answer:

'Of course you do... All Hollanders like wild duck.'

He held the menu in his hands. Impressive workman's hands, strong and relaxed with tapering fingers.

'And a good wine,' he said, 'I like wild duck with a good red wine.'

He really did go for this tasty duck and so did I.

Once he had said: 'An artist should be a man first.' That he is, and it's no wonder that I happened to meet many women in New York art circles who, all of them it seemed, had known him well, and who invariably each had something to say about him. He has had a great power of attraction on women and they conversely on him.

'... but he isn't the marrying kind.'

While we were having dinner he suddenly asked me: 'Do they still say 'jongens onder mekaar' in Holland?'(Expression of the idea 'Just between, or among, the boys'.)

This was the first time he had spoken Dutch. He had a good laugh when I confirmed this. De Kooning had arrived in America without being able to speak a word of English.

'I picked it up from the streets, from my colleagues, from the New York signs, in the movies, and in my reading of the newspapers.'

He had to suppress his native language to learn the foreign language as fast and as well as possible.

'Now that I'm sixty, Dutch comes back, you see. I think I had to forget it.'

De Kooning says 'tink' and 'ting'. As in 'Anyting you can tink of is a ting but whatever a ting is, it's always someting else.'

After dinner we went to the house in East Hampton he'd bought eight years earlier; an old, locally-styled house of wood, painted white. The walls of the large living-room are white. No paintings upon the walls, though a few small, framed prints do hang there. In a corner sits a TV. We sit at a low, round table. At this table De Kooning works when he gets back from his studio - drawing while sitting looking at TV.

'The mother of Lisbeth my daughter, who's thirteen now, is the one who did all the decorating here. I thought she and the little girl would come and live here with me, but it didn't work out that way. They come to visit me every weekend now.'

And then with a jocular smile he went on:

'Once I was in Rome, and at a party there I met an American painter of my age, dignified and well-dressed. I love to be well-dressed. He had a nice wife, and a son in college. They were making the rounds of museums and ruins; they knew about all there was to see and enjoyed looking at it intelligently. When I was young I expected to turn into that sort of man, but somehow it didn't happen.'

As he says this he doesn't seem to be sorry about it. I asked him why he went to America in 1926, and not to Paris, as did many young artists of this time. He answered:

'When we went to the Academy in Rotterdam - doing painting, decorating, making a living - young artists were not interested in painting *per se*. We used to call that "good for men with beards." And the idea of a palette, with colors on it, was rather silly. At that time

20

we were influenced by the de Stijl group. The idea of being a modern person wasn't really being an artist in the sense of being a painter. So it wasn't illogical to come to America instead of going to Paris. Also, being young, I really didn't understand the nature of painting. I really intended to become an applied artist. I mean, it was more logical to be a designer or a commercial artist. I didn't intend to become a painter - that came later.'

The first signs of unemployment manifested themselves in Holland in the middle 1920's. America was the 'Land of Opportunity', where anything could happen. And De Kooning, driven by a sense of adventure that was later to make him one of the greatest painters of our times, entered the New World.

'I didn't expect that there were any artists here. We never heard in Holland that there were artists in America. There was still the feeling that this was where an individual could get places and become well off, if he worked hard; while art, naturally, was in Europe. When I had been here for about six months or a year I found out that there were artists here too. There was Greenwich Village; there was a whole tradition in painting and in poetry. I just didn't know about it, and it must have directed me back to interests I had when I was fourteen, fifteen, sixteen years old. When you're about nineteen and twenty, you really want to go up in the world and you don't mind giving up art.'

But there is more. His parents being divorced, he'd one time be shuttled off to his father's, another time back to his mother's house. His father dealt in wines, beers and soft drinks.

'He was the one who gave me thirty guilders - when I got some fake papers to go to America, with friends of mine from the harbor. He never cared much for me. His work and drinking took so much time that he didn't see me very often. But after I'd been in New York for some time, I wrote him a letter telling him that I'd been learning a lot, and that I'd gotten so intelligent that at least I could understand *him*.'

His father wrote him back, one short letter with contents as follows: 'Well okay, boy, sometimes that's how it goes in life.' He's never heard anything from him since, and he's been long dead. He would very much like to see him once again. We were drinking; De Kooning less than I.

'I shouldn't drink *too much*; I'm not on the wagon, but it's better for me not to now, anyhow, I want to work... You know, I'm really a *terrible* drinker, I can't stop. I get lost, totally lost; I become inhuman, a beast. And the hangovers, including the moral ones... it's awful.'

And right after that: 'My mother is still alive. She's nearly ninety now. I sometimes get the idea that she's immortal. She has been here; she's lived in Hampton Bay - at Franz Kline's place... No, not with me. She's quite a character, you know.'

De Kooning, although he had made two visits to Europe, had never returned to Rotterdam.

'Women have always been a preoccupation of Bill's,' said Elaine. 'Bill's own mother, who still lives in Rotterdam, is a real doll, but she has a ferocious aspect!'

Elaine de Kooning said this with reference to the shocking 'Women' series of paintings of the 1950's, with which De Kooning had earned his great, albeit contro-versial, reputation. A series of demoniacal portraits of women which have nonetheless been made not without humor. For humor plays a major role in his work. And humor in his conversations. He can laugh about himself. 'The ambiguity of reality', the distance he can take through it from what is happening around him, makes this humor an essential of his life and work. And then Thomas Hess, one of the earliest admirers of and great-est authorities on De Kooning, says quite rightly:

'In the early *Women*, tenderness changes to high-comedy. The *Men* are abandoned for glittering duchesses who lapse into funny poses and have a weak-ness for cock-eyed hats. De Kooning's Woman is of course, the White Goddess, and readers interested in her aunts are referred to archaic Boetia and the lost cities of Mycenae, Knossos and their Tarascan settlements, to the Theban goddess Nut and Marilyn Monroe, Aztec dolls, Kali, Artemis-Isis, Willendorf, Jigg's Maggie. But she is more interesting in herself. As the artist expands and deepens the theme, a woman in a chair, on a city street corner, enthroned on her inside-outside porch or wharf, becomes an architecture of colonnades and domes, a landscape with a back yard on Tenth Street growing from her ocean beaches. After the initial shock of her appearance wears off, she sits next to us on a bus, or is seen waving at someone behind us in a restaurant.'

De Kooning himself says: 'About *Woman III* an old critic once said: "I'm familiar with her, she looks just like one of my acquaintances."'

This critic was Clement Greenberg, who had recognized De Kooning's talent as early as 1928.

'I had a painting then called *Woman-Naked-Table-Flower*. He told me I had a sense of humor. He really had me picked out.' And laughing in advance at his own joke, he added: 'Humor sneaks in.'

The TV was on, and every now and then we'd have a brief look, at a musical.

'Musicals, oh boy, what musicals I saw. From them I learned a lot, about the language I mean, and as I say - from the newspapers at first, and later on from literature.'

What writers does he like?

'In the beginning, already in Rotterdam, Dostoyefski was my favorite, but later on, here: Faulkner, Joyce, Flaubert, and Thomas Wolfe, especially *Look Homeward Angel* and *You Can't Go Home Again*.'

Faulkner's *Light in August*, especially, has haunted him for years.

'There are two men talking in a barn; and off to the side in the doorway stands Joe Christmas the half-breed in what I imagine to be a kind of zoot suit,' says De Kooning, 'I'd like to paint Joe Christmas one of these days. And then there's the movies of course. I'm crazy about films. Tom Mix, Hoot Gibson, Asta Nielsen, Charlie Chaplin... Later on I read Sartre, Heidegger, Kierkegaard. I agree very much with the existentialists. But that came later.'

Now we turn back to 1926 and his arrival to America.

'In August of that year we arrived at Newport News, Virginia. I was a wiper in the engine room. My sailor

friends shouted: Look, Bill, America. And what I saw was
a sort of Holland, lowlands, just like back home. What
the hell did I want to go to America for? But anyhow I
could get on a coaster to Boston as a stoker, and then go
by train to Rhode Island and by boat to South Street,
New York. As I remember it: No skyscrapers - they had
disappeared in the mist. I took the Barclay Street ferry to
Hoboken. My sailor friends knew the Dutch settlement
there, and they brought me to the Dutch Seamen's
Home, a sort of boarding house. Thanks to them the
landlady gave me three weeks' credit. It was a neat little
place, and very clean. I like that. Here's some advice: Just
keep your place clean and there'll always be a guy who'll
come by and take you out to a good dinner. Three days
later I was a housepainter, and got nine dollars a day,
a nice salary for that time. In one week I could buy a
new suit, black, for Sundays, low-belt trousers, nice
workman's clothes, for I didn't want to be different. I do
like a fine suit and a nice tie. [It's a fact that De Kooning
always has appeared at openings in a trim suit with a
nifty tie.] In three weeks I could pay off my rent and had
new underwear and socks. And can you imagine that a
few years before this I'd worked with some friends in
Belgium, for three months, Antwerp and Brussels, all
sorts of jobs, and after three months of crazy work
I couldn't even buy one pair of socks. Well here I painted
houses the first year. What the hell - if you can paint
you can paint houses too. One year of this and then
I went to Manhattan, to Greenwich Village, and met my
first friends, like Arshile Gorky the painter and Edward
Denby the poet. Still had to do odd jobs, but also got a
studio of my own where I could work evenings.'

25

Arshile Gorky was a fantastic man, a colorful figure who bounded around in his Don Cossack uniform. A good painter, too, who had had a lot of influence on De Kooning. When people blamed him for that after Gorky's death, De Kooning wrote a letter to ARTNews, of which the following is a passage: 'When about fifteen years ago I walked into Arshile's studio for the first time, the atmosphere was so beautiful that I got a little dizzy, and when I came to, I was bright enough to take the hint immediately... I am glad that it is about impossible to get away from his influence, as long as I keep it with myself, I'll be doing all right.'

And Edward Denby wrote about his relationship to influences in general:

'As he struggled in the early forties with his unfinishable pictures, day by day De Kooning was also finding out what further concepts some other theory could suggest to him. He found out what it meant by using it. Pressed to join a cause: "That's your status quo," he shouted, "I'm not serving anybody's status quo."'

De Kooning stood free of trends, political convictions, ideas about what American art had to be, ideas which, besides, were always changing. As Thomas Hess has written:

'American painting, since the time of Benjamin West, has been the Dark Horse of the European art world. Europeans always had demanded, and Americans, being Europeans, tried to fulfill the idea of an American culture - whether *Pantisocracy* for Coleridge or *Amerika* for Kafka. The Romantic notion of the American Dark Horse finally "making its move" at the turn to "win" a race be-

26

came, by repetition, an American chauvinistic habit - almost a cultural tic - which De Kooning has called "Eating John Brown's Body" (i.e., coming from nowhere to become, by proclamation, The Champion). But it always was obvious to artists like De Kooning and Gorky that such "moves" were futile and that modern art is international and cosmopolitan.'

In reference to this, De Kooning has stated: 'The history of art is separate from all history but connected. It meets with everything else, but it has its own constants.'

And about this 'dark horseness' and America and Gorky he had much to tell me.

'I met a lot of artists - but then I met Gorky. I had some training in Holland, quite a training, the Academy. Gorky didn't have that at all. He came from no place; he came here when he was sixteen, from Tiflis in Georgia, with an Armenian upbringing. And for some mysterious reason he knew lots more about painting and art - he just knew it by nature - things I was supposed to know and feel and understand - he really did it better. He had an extraordinary gift for hitting the nail on the head, very remarkable. So I immediately attached myself to him and we became very good friends. It was nice to be foreigners meeting in some new place. Of course, New York is really like a Byzantine city - it is very natural too. I mean, that is probably one of the reasons why I came myself, without knowing. When I was a child I was very interested in America; it was romantic... cowboys and Indians. Even the shield, the medieval shield they have

27

with the stars on top and the stripes on the bottom, was almost like the heraldic period of the Crusaders, with the eagle; as a child I used to be absolutely fascinated by this image. Now that is all over. It's not so much that I'm an American: I'm a New Yorker. I think we have gone back to the cities, and I feel much more in common with artists in London or Paris. It is a certain burden, this American-ness. If you come from a small nation, you don't have that. When I went to the Academy and I was drawing from the nude, *I* was making the drawing, not Holland. I feel sometimes an American artist must feel, like a baseball player or something, a member of a team writing American history. I think it is kind of nice that at least part of the public is proud that they have their own sports and things like that - and why not their own art? I think it's wonderful that you know where you come from; I mean you know, if you are American you are an American!'

Then, beaming his jocular grin again, he summed up with 'If I painted in Russia, I'd probably be another type of painter because of the environment there. Who knows, but I'd still paint!'

De Kooning's whole development is a single demon-stration of independence. He had learned his occupation well, but he was of no school, he formed no school, he remained changingly and effectively himself. He did with himself what he used to ask of his students at Black Mountain College.

'Take some plaster-of-Paris and make a ball out of it, but really *round*; try to get it so round that it looks like a perfect sphere when the sun strikes its surface. Okay, you do this, and holding it up to the light you see some rough spots. So you sandpaper these down - as smooth as you can - and hold it to the light again: Still not round; not perfectly round. To get it that way you could spend a lifetime. I know this is a grueling exercise, terribly hard training, but it's necessary, it's Zen Buddhistic. Later on it comes to you that "perfect roundness" is nothing but an idea - the illusion of roundness. Industry makes perfect balls - so they tell us. But, what the hell, we know nothing about *that*, and so what.'

De Kooning is an artist who in his work is continually being confronted with the problems of the creative process, of the technique of painting itself, such as: how to evoke the planes, surfaces and spaces - abstract or figurative -, and the mode of what can and cannot be done.

'Certain artists and critics attacked me for painting the *Women*, but I felt that this was their problem, not mine. I don't really feel like a non-objective painter at all. Today some artists feel they have to go back to the figure, and that word "figure" becomes such a ridiculous omen; if you pick up some paint with your brush and make somebody's nose with it, this is rather ridiculous when you think about it, theoretically or philosophically. It's really absurd to make an image, like a human image, with paint, today, when you think about it, since we have this problem of doing or not doing it. But then all of a sudden it was even more absurd not to do it. So I fear that I have to follow my desires...

I wasn't concerned to get a particular kind of feeling. I look at them now and they seem vociferous and ferocious. I think it had to do with the idea of the idol, the oracle, and above all the hilariousness of it. I do think that if I don't look upon life that way, I won't know how to keep on being around.

I cut out a lot of mouths. First of all, I thought every-thing ought to have a mouth. Maybe it was like a pun. Maybe it's sexual. But whatever it is, I used to cut out a lot of mouths and then I painted those figures and then I put the mouth more or less in the place where it was supposed to be. It always turned out to be very beautiful and it helped me immensely to have the real thing.'

It was around 1940 that De Kooning first started set-ting up paintings with letters, merely a few alphabetical symbols, on the canvas. (We might find a *zot*, or *hello*, among other word possibilities.) Elaine de Kooning once remarked on one such instance: 'I can almost remember the exact words  -  one like *hope* clear across the top, and one like *man* across the bottom.' She explains, too, how he transmuted the letters into other forms and ob-jects, while 'obliterating' them:

'At the top, see how the first letter became the win-dow shape he always used. Next is a loop that was part of the *o*, and then the *p* has become an apple with the downstroke making the leg of a table. The *e* has become a floor lamp seen from above. At the bottom, the capital *M* became a sort of hand  -  you know at that time Bill would look at his thumb and make a shape on the can-vas. Then he would say to me: "You have to start some-where." The rest of the shapes at the bottom were also suggested by the letters.'

And De Kooning went on on how he had gotten 'some-where' by expanding the spaces around a basic form into an *action* - 'I did it with the mouth. Maybe the grin - it's rather like the Mesopotamian idols, they always stand up straight, looking to the sky with this smile, like they were astonished about the forces of nature you feel, not about problems they had with one another. That I was very conscious of - the smile was something to hang onto... I wouldn't know what to do with the rest, with the hands, maybe, or some gesture, and then in the end I failed. But then it didn't bother me because I had, in the end, given it up; I felt it was really an accomplish-ment. I took the attitude that I was going to succeed, and I also knew that this was just an illusion. I never was interested in how to make a good painting. For many years I was not interested in making a good paint-ing - as one might say: "Now this is really a good paint-ing" or "perfect work." I didn't want to pin it down at all... I was interested in that before, but I found out it was not my nature. I didn't work on it with the idea of perfection, but to see how far one could go - but not with the idea of really doing it. With anxiousness and dedication to fright maybe, or ecstasy, like the *Divine Comedy*, to be a performer: to see how long you can stay on the stage with that imaginary audience.'

It's wonderful to watch and listen to De Kooning talking, and how he goes about it, covering a subject from all aspects in a single stretch - and wrapping it up with a burst of laughter, a joke and a grin. Like De Kooning, himself an man of many brilliant and no fixed ideas,

Harold Rosenberg the critic, says quite rightly: 'He is an ideologist's man, but anti-ideological.'

And the motto here, what Bill has said in short, is 'The artist takes art as he finds it.'

When I asked him what influence philosophy might cast on his work, he answered: 'It's like a girl; you either take the hint or you don't.' And after consolidating some observations about this significant subject, one of his favorites, esthetics, with illustrations from the extensive series of Women he has made over the years, after this, about which we had a good laugh, we somehow got into cosmological questions, which, it is said, sometimes scare or bore him... especially when it comes to 'space'.

'*Space*. Oh boy, we could go on for ever exploring the space of science, but I'll tell you something: If I stretch my arms next to the rest of myself... and wonder where my fingers are, I have all the space I need as a painter! The stars of astronomical space I use as buttons on my jacket.'

Then came the late news on TV, during and about which he makes no comment; turns that off now and brings out a book of reproductions  -  Bernini  -  to show me.

'*The Ecstasy of Saint Theresa*. You see that face?! Fantastic hmm? And corny. Any part of that statue could be something else. The clothes could be leaves, but then he puts that face on top, and that's "it"... as if she's coming. And that foot at the bottom  -  fantastic... He had the "it", the "oomph". You have to have it, you have to "oomph around" with your work.'

Then out of the blue:

'D'ya know the book *Two Serious Ladies* by Jane Bowles? Well, those ladies are my "Women". In an humorous or philosophical sense they're nut-ting. Or those Saint Theresa's of Gertrude Stein in her play for saints in three acts. Now these are really Theresa's! When Theresa I meets Theresa II, it goes something like:

"Oh hello! How are you?"

"Very well thanks! And you?"

"Just fine!...isn't it a nice day."

"Yes indeed! Today it's real nice."

and you know that this is "nuttingness", "no content". After all, when you're not a philosopher, you can't sit around with a tank in your room.'

And then he went to bed.

*   *   *

The next morning, while I was still taking a shower, Bill was already in the kitchen, and shouted to me: 'Bert, do you want ham and eggs scrambled? Or fried eggs sunny-side up?' De Kooning seemed to be in a splendid mood, after only three or four hours of sleep.

I went to the kitchen, a country kitchen, nice and large, and bill greeted me with my book *De gestalte der stem* (The Shape of the Voice) in hand. 'Listen to this, I'll read it to you.' And he read a few pages in faultless Dutch. Perfect rhythms, pronunciation and accent. I told him so and he was glad about it.

'You know, now that I'm sixty Dutch words come back to me, but I still dream in English.'

A little later, we were leaving the house for his studio, on bicycles.

'I like cycling along the lonely beaches, and to ride over to neighbors' places for visits. You know, this life of a country boy has started to grow on me, I really like it.'

Then he focused my attention to our land-and-seascape surroundings.

'You are a poet. So before seeing my studio, you should see Louse Point. The beach, the sea, the ocean. It's really a little bit of Holland.'

A crisp, winter wind rolled across the beach as Bill and I stood there at Louse Point, Long Island, that cold morning. A beach like Holland's as we look out to sea now, the same grey ocean as it might have looked from the Dutch coast when Bill set forth over forty years age to 'discover America'. The sea before us, and not far behind a wide inlet, a bay. This whole scene, essentially very Dutch. Some fishermen, their black-jacketed backs bent intently over their poles, stood in a row fishing on the beach. Bill commented:

'I've always been fascinated by water, you see. It reflects while you are reflecting. I see them everywhere, these people... here and at Sheep's-head Bay, Brooklyn. I don't give a damn about the fish. It's the water. I try to paint it like this, open, but then it ends up I have to put a boat in it too. I remember the epitaph on Shelley's tomb in Rome - I was with Gregory Corso when I saw this - it said something like:

*"Here lie the remains of an English poet*
*Who wrote his name in water"...* the last line.'

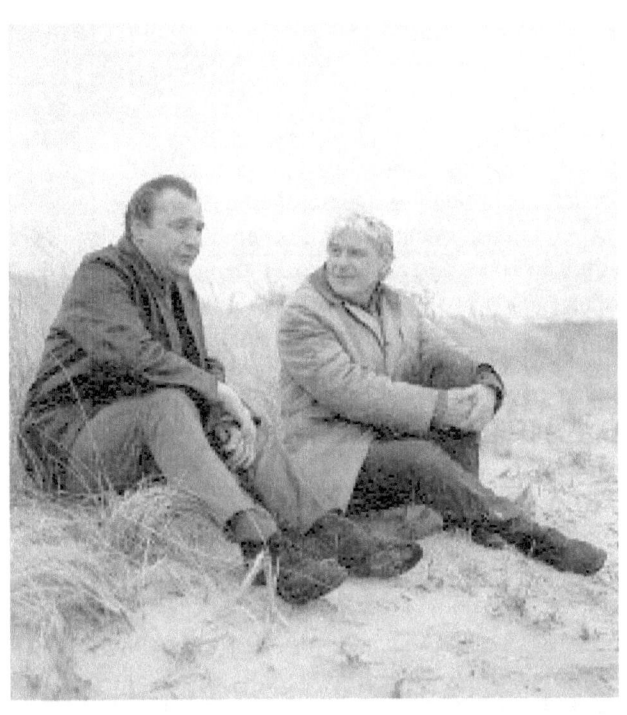

*Bert Schierbeek (left) and Willem de Kooning on Long Island (1967)*

As we then took an extended stroll along the strand, the salt air turned our talk to philosophy again, and Zen.

'Even before I knew philosophy I was interested in nothingness, emptiness, empty spaces and places. All those vacant lots of buildings demolished between decaying buildings in Manhattan, the open highways and all that. So when Corso had already seen enough - we were on the Via Appia, where the tombs ended - I said to him: No, no, let's go on and see some more of this. This has nothing to do with what people say about my being an abstract painter, but maybe I am an expressionist, after all. Anyhow, not even for a million dollars would I paint a tree, I can't...'

On the other hand, De Kooning's fascination for the details of line on the human figure is as Thomas Hess has remarked 'an obsessional attraction'. Bill was saying:

'I used to get so involved in drawing elusive things like noses. Imagine how the shadow falls on the fleshy part of a nose, and how are you going to render that with a hard pencil? These are the drawing problems that can drive you nuts, that you have to give up.'

And I thought of a drawing I'd seen that he's done of his former wife, Elaine. Something like some of Picasso's, in a way. A fantastic drawing - accurate, plastic, alive... with those staring eyes as only De Kooning can render them. These are eyes that are emotionally evocative of no particular place, of 'no environment' - of the void in which we live, dramatically. As Bill has said: 'Only that subject matter is valid which is tragic and timeless.'

Now we were sitting in the sand. The wind spread his grey hair across his forehead, and while his face was smiling, this wasn't so of his steel-blue eyes. It was the same jocular, reflective grin I'd seen so frequently the while we spent together. His at once aloof, expectant, anticipatory expression. It is open and closed; it is within and without; it's like an animal knowing nature and her forces, trusting in them as it has to live with it, wary of its treachery.

But then he laughed. Life is ambiguous, as is reality, as is truth quite unreliable. And as for what De Kooning has created: 'It's all very puzzling, but I'm not a puzzle,' he stated on one occasion.

And on the beach:

'Can you imagine what they once told me? "Your work is an exact expression of Einstein's United Field Theory." Well, naturally, this United Field Theory deals with the universe and I'm part of that, but what the hell, I always knew that.'

And with that we decided to leave the beach and its fishermen, and cycled at our leisure along the coastal road between the seashore and the bay on the way to his studio. The studio lies within a Dutchlike dunish landscape, very similar to Bergen, a seaside art-colony in Holland. We stopped halfway there to pick up a bottle of whisky and some beer.

The studio is situated in a natural bowl, or rather cup, in the dunes. We were approaching it now.

'This place is my own design - for living as well as the dealers... "ultra modern"... Not "in style" but for my style of living. I don't know when, if ever, it will be finished, like the pictures I paint. As you see, I have a nostalgia for the New. All those rotten old lofts I lived in were like "The House of Usher" - falling. I wanted something totally new - none of that "Home Sweet Home"-crap. It's more a continuing "self-extending action" of mine than a home, but carried out by others... I hope it becomes one of my "unfinished masterpieces".'

It is his four-dimensional 'Abstract Landscape' in concrete, steel, wood and glass. From the outside, as seen in the forms of the wooden balcony and of the slant of the wings of the roof sections, its structural lines swoop and soar like a monumental seagull over the dune-scape. These lines are an architectural extension of his sweeping brushstrokes, as in *Merritt Parkway*, lines that evoke not only a dominantly-impressive, environment-in-motion image, the Highway, i.e., trips to and from the city, but that greater sensation of 'no place'-in-particular of New York City itself.

The studio has indeed been a house building according to the many and perpetually-permutating plans of its designer. We stepped inside and Bill started showing me around.

'You see? A dwelling-studio,' and my eyes fell upon the 'composed curve' of a staircase. 'It leads up to the bedrooms,' said he, 'for a ball with beautiful women.' Five of them, five rooms up there. The upstairs apartment was at first intended for his daughter and her mother.

'But... oh well - I'm not pretending to be an architect. I know this place would drive most "modernistic" architects out of their minds, but I like it, in spite of the headaches. And I think Frank Lloyd Wright would feel quite at home in it.'

From the upstairs-apartment end of the building there's a sort of bridge, where the captain can survey his colossal sun-deck below.

'This house does have something of a ship about it, hmm, Bert?' I nodded in recognition, the staircase-bridge, the decklike platforms, the hold-spacious studio. I gazed astounded at the extent of the ceiling's highest junctures, well up to 45 feet, and the light of January drenched the interior from both the long, tall 'gallery' sides of glass-louvred windows.

'And a certain air of Holland too, hmm? You know how it is in Rotterdam. As a kid I always hung around ships, the water, and the way the sea reflects the sky, the light here, it's all so much like Holland.'

I had to agree, and we walked around the spacious and well-lighted studio area. The floor littered with oil-swirled sheets of paper he used for testing ideas. Colors in groups of white, heavy-duty cups and bowls are ranged out on long work-tables. Clean brushes are lined up on the floor. One table holds hundreds of boxes of tubes of oil-paint; the basic ingredient of his special recipes - a delicious menu of slow-drying hues. 'Completed' paintings of the present series are stacked along the walls.

Adjoining the studio, under the bedrooms, is the large living-room, with a gracefully curved, plastered, black-painted fireplace extending to the ceiling-roof. It's a stately torso of Woman, a majestic statueform in itself.

'I think I'll repaint it  -  it's too black.'

And he says on the window-frames: 'They need some re-working too,' and of the back door:

'Maybe I'll move that a little to the right. You know what it is to be an amateur architect.' (I had told him of my own little house that I built on a little Spanish island.) 'Well, what happens to me,' he said, 'is that most of my ideas, my better ideas it's sad to say, seem to come when most of the house is finished.'

I'd venture to say that only his kitchen  -  as spacious, well-equiped and well-furnished as it is  -  will remain unchanged.

'The kitchen is all right.' It is furnished and built simply and well; the sink is mounted firmly within a solid wood encasement and there is a rustic table that serves its purpose.

We stepped out the back door for a breath of brisk air. Surrounding the house is a fairly wide, neat, but not entirely flat, lawn; in the back there's a little round summerhouse, 'my temple, for tea-drinking when it's nice and warm out here,' says Bill. The border of the front lawn is a row of large, eloquent stones.

'Long Island's answer to Stonehenge. They've been brought over here by the truckloads.'

Suddenly he chuckles and says:

'Oh boy, when I think of all these building costs, I start feeling like Caruso when he got his first contract; he said: "If I really earned this much, I'll just have to sing better next year."'

Then, looking with reflective fascination at his most imposing creation:

'Well, let's just say it's my work-in-process and I like to play around with alterations now and then.'

It's original, it's a De Kooning, it'll never be finished.

* * *

Next morning, it's ten, and Bill starts a day of painting. One of the newest *Women* series on easel, upside down. De Kooning looks at it from a distance, nodding his satisfaction.

'This is a painting I've been working on these last two months. I've made two or three major changes on it every day. I do a lot of scraping off. There must be twenty stages to this one already, twenty layers of painting I've gone over.'

He approaches the easel; its legs are sunk into a deep trough.

'I don't like to climb steps when I'm working, so I made this slot. The easel is constructed in a way that the painting can be turned around any time I want to approach it from another aspect. I don't care to bend over to look at it through my legs upside-down.'

There are two tables, covered with cups of paint, handy to the easel.

'I got an idea for preparing colors that suit my particular way of painting one day at Howard- Johnson's, the ice cream-makers. Then also I knew a guy, Giorgio Spalenta, who was a sort of mystic about numbers. At that time he was a superhuman problem-solver for me; he helped me figure out a way to mix colors just the way I want them. Like this color here, see? The color of boiled liver; remember how it looked in the Dutch marketplaces? I think I had to blend about seven colors to get it. It made me feel like an alchemist. Isn't it nice? I've been making a lot of off-beat hues lately... to get rid of those hard reds, greens, yellows and blues that you find in the displays. I don't like them anymore. Nor the flesh colors: the same old soupy palette of colors: white, orange, yellow and blue. But you know, some latter-day art theorists were saying that there are certain things the artist ought not to paint anymore. And when I thought about it, it's really too silly  -  if Gauguin made figures yellow, and Picasso painted some blue ones, what the hell, I was going to use flesh color. After all: flesh was the reason why oil-painting was invented! Anyhow, my new flesh tones are something else.'

And then he went on with his painting. He took a brush with green, dabbed on a green spot... then a swift wavelike stroke of green... and then he scraped the greater part of this off again, and started using a violet. He backed off from the easel to get some distance on his painting. Dissatisfied, he now scraped off most of the violet. This left a satin-smooth, thin layer  -  and this he did like.

Sometimes, when the natural properties of color do not bring about the textures and moods that he is seeking, De Kooning spreads sheets of newsprint over part of the moist paint surface, jiggles them slightly, and removes them carefully, achieving a kind of whipped-cream frothiness. In some cases he leaves the newspaper upon the canvas, paints over it and thus it gets embodied into the picture.

De Kooning took up with his favorite subject again.

'You know now I'm going back to what I used to do - to women - and now I can do it better: I feel competent, yet I get flustered enough to feel exited.'

I saw him work through several rhythmically-diverse phases of this painting, *The Visit*, during my stay at De Kooning's. But as one critic remarked, '...the variety of tempo in his work does not damage the continuity of it.'

And Bill says:

'Painting isn't the first visual thing that reaches your retina, it's what is behind it. I'm not interested in "abstracting", or taking things out, or reducing painting to design, form, line and color. I paint the way I do because I can keep putting more and more things in - like drama, pain, anger, love, a figure, a horse, my ideas of space. Through your eyes it becomes an emotion or an idea. It doesn't matter if it differs from mine, as long as it comes from the painting, which has its own integrity and intensity. And don't ever forget: Nothing is positive about art, except that it is a word.'

De Kooning worked on, all morning long. He didn't drink. He had said to me: 'Drink all you want. There's ice in the ice-box. Put some ice in your drink - it's nice, it's the American way.'

For lunch we had bread and cheese and some wine. And then De Kooning went back to and on with his painting - until sunset.

'I don't paint by artificial light anymore.'

The afternoon now over, we leave the studio to go and buy two TV-dinners at a local supermarket.

That day De Kooning had done a good deal of painting and change-making - sometimes humming a song, sometimes while whistling, sometimes taking some distance from his painting to stare into the distances he wanted to see in that painting that bugged him. 'Content is a glimpse...

                    ...It's very tiny...

                                        ...It's nearly nothing...'

Sometimes he would walk back to an old wicker armchair, sit down and look at his painting, take out a cigarette and smoke it, and as I was there he would talk. For he does like to talk, and now and then to have long conversations with friends.

'That's why I like to be among writers as well as artists. I don't think that writers are necessarily more intelligent or in general have more to say than artists, but I find talking with them very stimulating. Some-times I could say of myself that I paint with a good ear, because their talk, the words they use, made a picture in my mind. I got together with Edward Denby a lot, he's a good friend of mine, a poet, and we had many a long talk. He was one of the first artists I met in the Village. And another good friend from those days was John O'Hara, also a poet...'

For a moment he was very quiet:
'O'Hara had to do with the Museum of Modern Art, and we were very good friends. He was killed out here by a car - run over on the beach, a few months ago. It was terrible. I couldn't work for weeks... He was a very good friend, you see, and when this kind of friend dies you just stop... It seems at such times that everything is meaningless - whatever you're doing, anything you see, or think about - it's a total void, a terrible thing. Well of course, a few weeks later you go on - it's part of your life. You want to live, you keep searching for something, so you keep trying to paint it, but in the end you die, anyhow - and that's a sort of failure.'

What's remarkable about Bill's talk is his always mellow mixture of reflective thought with jocularity:
'Insofar as we understand the universe - if it can be understood - our doings must have some desire for order in them; but from the point of view of the universe, they must be very grotesque.'

Now we arrive at his 'Old' house - to which he always returns after a day's work. There to eat and sleep. And when there are no visitors, to make some sketches of figures while looking at TeeVee.
And this evening there is a visitor, a neighbor, who'd brought him some fresh oysters and cooked them for us.

And we ate the oysters and the TV-dinners en we enjoyed them. Bill does enjoy a good meal, and good restaurants:

'Oh boy - the meals we had in New York were sometimes fantastic. I don't go there so often anymore. I'm settled out here now. All I care about is to be able to work without being bothered by people. There's yet some time to accomplish something, and that's what I want to do. Nature, you see, is chaotic, and all we can hope for is to put some order into ourselves. When a man ploughs his field at the right moment, it means exactly that.'

After supper we went to sit in the large living-room, turned on the TV, looked for some news, and continued our conversation. And because Bill likes talking, this portrait in words has been realized to a great degree by him.

Some people talk too much; not De Kooning, however, because he's always twisting your nose, or the nose of a recent theory, or his own nose grown somewhat with his talks. He has a tremendous sense of, or better feeling for, humor. And with that you can sit and enjoy talking with him for hours on end. And you will oftentimes hear him say: '...while on the other hand...' or 'from that point of view...' or 'if you consider this aspect...' For there are many ways to approach reality. And his reality is 'ambiguous', the opposite of 'fixed', meaning 'going around' something.

'The logic of De Kooning's work lies not in its rational consistency but in the artist's unending struggle with painting and its possibilities. Each confrontation of the drawing board or canvas is a singular situation calling for a new act - and the act and the artist are one. The web of energies he has woven between his painting and his living precludes the formation of any terminal idea. No one could be more remote either from the 'pure' artist, who paints what he conceives to be the essence of painting, or from the correct artist, who produces what is demanded by the history of art or by society. Throughout his career De Kooning has resisted every species of ideology - esthetic, social, and philosophical. Picking up Kierkegaard's book, *Purity of Heart Is To Will One Thing*, his response to the title was, 'The idea makes me sick'. His own unexpressed standard is the standard of the mountain climber or the boxer, that is, a trained sense of immediate rightness...' as Harold Rosenberg the critic observed. And to hear him talk and see him paint as I did is to know that the foregoing is true. He never has been able to 'finish' a painting. That's why all his paintings are 'open'; they reach no 'conclusions'; they are part of his own never-ending development. They are 'acts' which call for further acts. And because he never could finish a painting - even as his energies were accumulating - he was often living under nearly unbearable tensions. 'Now... I'll just stop,' he said to me one of these times.

That night we got to talking about the 1930's - during which he'd been doing odd jobs by day and his painting in the evening.

'You know, I'll never forget those years, the Depression, and Franklin D. Roosevelt, he put an end to it.' He

47

went to a bookshelf, picked out a dusty, paperbound volume and located a passage. 'Listen to what Roosevelt said,' and he read to me:

'"Nobody is going to starve in this country. It seems equally plain that no business which depends on paying less than living wages has any right to continue. By business I mean all workers - the white collar class as well as the man in overalls. And by wages I mean more than a bare subsistence level, I mean wages of decent living."'

It is clear that De Kooning felt moved in reading those words.

'We did jobs through the WPA (Works Progress Administration), part of The New Deal, and we got our deal from the Federal Art Program. All artists had work, and got paid for it. The painters were affiliated with the house-painters, the sculptors with the bricklayers, and so on. And as Roosevelt had promised, we got "decent" wages; and artists could do the work in their own studies. For an artist those were extraordinary times, when one could live modestly. I met all kinds of people in the same boat. It's sort of crazy, too, when you think that it took the Depression to make it possible to be a full-time artist... From then on I painted full-time.'

Then he smiled and said: 'But, anyhow, by now I'd gotten into painting as a way of living, and I was going to go on with it full-time. There was money to buy paint, but sometimes only for black and white household enamels. I was making quite a few black-and-white paintings at that time - which people were calling 'abstractions'. But then after a while I got to using

48

colors again. We learned things about color from Hans Hoffman; he had a lot to say on color theory. And there were several other Europeans who influenced American painting in those days, those who were war refugees and immigrants in the late thirties and early forties. We learned a lot from them, but also we were becoming more and more confident and conscious of our own accomplishments. And when I say 'we' I mean, among others: Pollock, Rothko, Franz Kline, Clifford Still, Robert Motherwell, Hans Hoffman, Gorky - all of us friends... And, oh yes, I'll have to tell you about our Club. We wanted a place of our own to meet regularly and talk about everything that was of interest to us. So five of us got together one Friday night in 1949 at the Waldorf Cafeteria on 6th Avenue and 8th Street; and the next Friday night was up to twenty. Twenty of us, the 'charter members', who paid $ 20 a piece, and we called it "The Club". It was a nice gang. Philip Pavia, the guy who owned the cafeteria, paid the rest. We had parties, and held lectures for artists there - by architects, musicians, Zen Buddhists, existentialists, even a priest. We each paid 75c per lecture. At first all twenty of us had to agree on bringing in a new member. But that didn't work so well because there was always someone voting against it. Then we decided that that should require two votes, and that worked better. Our 'charter' was: No program, no background, no future - always *in the flux*."

This is typical of De Kooning; he is an 'adventurer in chaos', and knows instinctively that 'the will to a system is a lack of integrity,' as Nietzsche has said. And apropos of art and artists, this same philosopher-poet also observed that 'One has to accustom the eye to calmness, to patience, to letting things come up to it; to postpone judgment, to learn to go around it and grasp each particular datum from all sides.'

Even his earlier paintings, most of men, foreshadow those complex concepts of 'no environment' he has most fully developed in his first, made-in-the-city series of Women. Referring to this earlier work, he remarked:

'It could be that then I was painting the woman in man. Art isn't a wholly masculine occupation, you know. I am aware that some critics would take this to be an admission of latent homosexuality. But if I painted *beautiful* women, exclusively as beautiful, would that make me a non-homosexual? I like beautiful women, in the flesh  -  even as models in magazines. Women irritate me sometimes. Maybe I painted that irritation in the first "Woman" series I did. What about that "Marilyn Monroe" I made? [The hyper-blonde sensation of his 1956 opening.] I don't know. I was just painting a picture and suddenly there she was. Someone asked if this might be subconscious desire. Subconscious, hell! But, you can never really know for sure about things. For instance, in those days I was going to some very fashionable parties, and there was one where I saw this particularly beautiful woman, the way she was dressed, fantastic, very elegant with a pearl necklace and all, and... I went over to her and said: "My god, you must be a Million-dollar girl." In a way, she was rather pleased that I could guess, but she insisted that I meet her husband, who turned out to be Nelson Rockefeller, the governor. And he was quite pleased too.'

By this time, the late 1950's, De Kooning had become - albeit unwillingly, and thanks to the mass-media - a focal point of public attention. As had many of his artist friends.

But it hadn't always been that way, as De Kooning explained:

'Before the war, America never really cared much for her own or *any*body's art and artists, and perhaps it is no exception, but the American public has to some extent learned a couple of basic things since then, as my friend Tom Hess has pointed out: one, that artists - even though they may be brilliant, and some maybe even a little arrogant sometimes - artists are, after all, human beings too, with pores and hairs... and two, that we take our work seriously, as seriously as any other profession, as a way of life that doesn't avoid the basic issues of life, but meets them head on. And we did that each in his own unique and individual way. Jackson Pollock broke the ice for us. He was really far-out for me then!'

But as a friend of Bill's told me later on, his first and decisive reaction to the explosion of American vanguard styles among his friends, particularly the 'abstracting of Expressionism', was: 'I'll beat them all.'

And at that highly self-assured moment in his development, he started work on his group of large and fantastically rich calligraphic figurations in color, including *Bolton Landing, Merritt Parkway*, an other oil paintings of his type which suggest the chaotic masses and mo-

tions in the No-man's land suspended between the city
and country lights.

* * *

The next morning he said: 'Let's go and visit Pollock's
grave.' Pollock is buried in a graveyard opposite De Kooning's Old house. We strolled in the morning sun and he
showed me around the cemetery. Before leaving he sur-
veyed the place with a rueful gaze, communicating the
pity of it all, this final failure, and remarked:
   'I liked him very much; I think I'll buy myself a plot
here, too.'

Then he went to his studio. And again he stood for
hours on end before this painting, *The Visit*, which had
been bugging him so for months. He had just applied a
considerably thick layer of paint to the canvas and now
was scraping most of it off as he so often does.
   'I scrape off pounds of paint, pounds. And it costs $ 3
a tube. But what can I do?'
   This is a regular part of the process he goes through,
though, this being bugged by it and scraping it off, a sort
of curettage.

De Kooning's paint never interferes with the painting.
As Thomas Hess has observed, it is there in an absolute
way, without 'style'.
   And Bill says: 'Well, I just didn't like those hard colors
anymore; I had to go from No-color to Color, from No-
paint to Paint, No-form to Form. Perhaps this connects
me with Zen, where you go from No-mind to Mind.

Maybe that's why I never keep track of my work. It actually keeps track of me; it haunts me; it's embarrassing. I don't keep catalogs... You have to start, over and again, from No-painting to Painting. And as far as I'm concerned, other people can scribble whatever they want about it!'

And then De Kooning takes a long, deep breath. His painterly changes of pace, the tempo of his living, his life 'style', does not interrupt the continuity of his work. He has made long paintings and short ones, fast ones and slow, to speak of the durations of their creation. And all his drawings and sketches are short ones, very short.

De Kooning has once said: 'It is disastrous to name ourselves.' For a name enslaves you and your possibilities. And De Kooning distances himself from the , for him too-limiting term 'abstract expressionism'. Though ultimately he will say: 'I'm more of an expressionist than anything else, if it needs a label.' An expressionist, however, will yield himself to his work, will not take a distance from it, will drown himself in it. And De Kooning acts in a different way. He anticipates, he observes, he figures his paintings out, and performing he paints this 'reasoning' in. Of this, Peter Hutchinson the artist, in a recent article he calls 'De Kooning's Reasoned Abstracts', says of some recent attempts to define De Kooning's work (the last one is Bill's own):

'Something is going on here and it does not sound very expressionist. "Style", "Luciferian pride", "structural underpinning", "heroic style", "grand style", "reasoned", "counterfeit" - these words are seldom if ever used in describing Expressionism. Expressionism is best "expressed" through the emotions, not through the mind. Style never takes precedence over emotion in expressionist paintings. The paint, however beautiful, is always sensed, or felt, more than reasoned in a logical way...'

And he proposes that the above words and phrases describe a Mannerist style; and that Mannerism in its various describable forms can and does occur in abstract or figurative works. It has manifested itself in several 'periods' of art history, on each occasion in a different disguise. Hutchinson defines other 'keynotes' of Mannerist painting as being,

'... High finish and emphasis on surface, detail, acid color, unnatural flesh tone, love of materials, artificiality - and above all, drama. Drama shown especially in gesture.'

Maybe that is what De Kooning's 'glimpse' is.

'How does one paint the legs of a woman on a bicycle? It's impossible - they move, and the motion and the light consume and remove the form...'

Hutchinson concludes his appreciative evaluation with:

'De Kooning is obviously too sophisticated a person to be an expressionist. I would postulate that he is too aware and too questioning to do classical art. It is an art of a day of changing belief.'

And I agree with him; De Kooning is far from being a Classicist. William Seitz wrote that 'His education bears a closer resemblance to a medieval journeyman of the guild.' His high standards of craftsmanship bear that out. Yet he has neither the group instinct of a guild member, nor does he try to hide behind what he has called the 'spiritual smokescreen' of some estheticians of modern art. At the end of one day's painting, Bill remarked:

'I don't think of art as something that "purifies" me; it seems I'm always involved in the melodrama of vulgarity.'

No - Bill will not serve any fixed conceptions of reality, or esthetics; he does not fit into anyone's pigeonhole; nor does he espouse any credo, political or professional, except that of the artist's will to freedom.

And that time when a young painter who'd run across him in the street and challenged him with: 'Doesn't it bother you to be so overrated?'

Bill responded:

'Not at all, but it does seem to bother you.'

No, art has become for him 'A way to avoid a way', and of becoming what one can be, despite the demands of society and environment.

The day I had to leave his hospitality, he said to me: 'I'll write you,' but I knew he wouldn't. For he has an aversion to writing or answering letters, to picking up the phone or paying taxes.

Now he stood there at the station platform, watching and waving as the train pulled out, his grey hair blowing in the wind, and he yelled 'tot ziens, so long!' but

he had already retreated into his personal distances.
A great painter and a great man, very much *in the flux*.